PIANO 101:

HOW TO PLAY THE PIANO LIKE A PRO IN 24 HOURS

By

JANE ANDERSON

INTRODUCTION.

Many people who wish to learn to play the piano in a day are discouraged by the idea of taking long, boring periods learning the music notes. The key thing you must do is put negative thoughts aside if you are really serious about getting to know how to play piano in a day, start with a clear mind. It takes time and of course, you have to pick up the music notes, on the other hand, it doesn't have to be that boring, and it surely doesn't have to take a lifetime before you can play on your own.

This eBook aims at helping you understand all important aspects of how to play the piano perfectly in 24 hours. All the necessary parameters are explained in layman's language. You will find in here techniques that help you succeed in things that you don't desire to do but aspire to achieve.

This eBook will guide your musical challenges in piano playing that you'd rather surrender to, bribe through, or resign than to face. The issues discussed pertaining how to mastering the notes and scales for your new venture will energize you through your most daunting tasks.

Ready Go!

The Sky is The Limit!

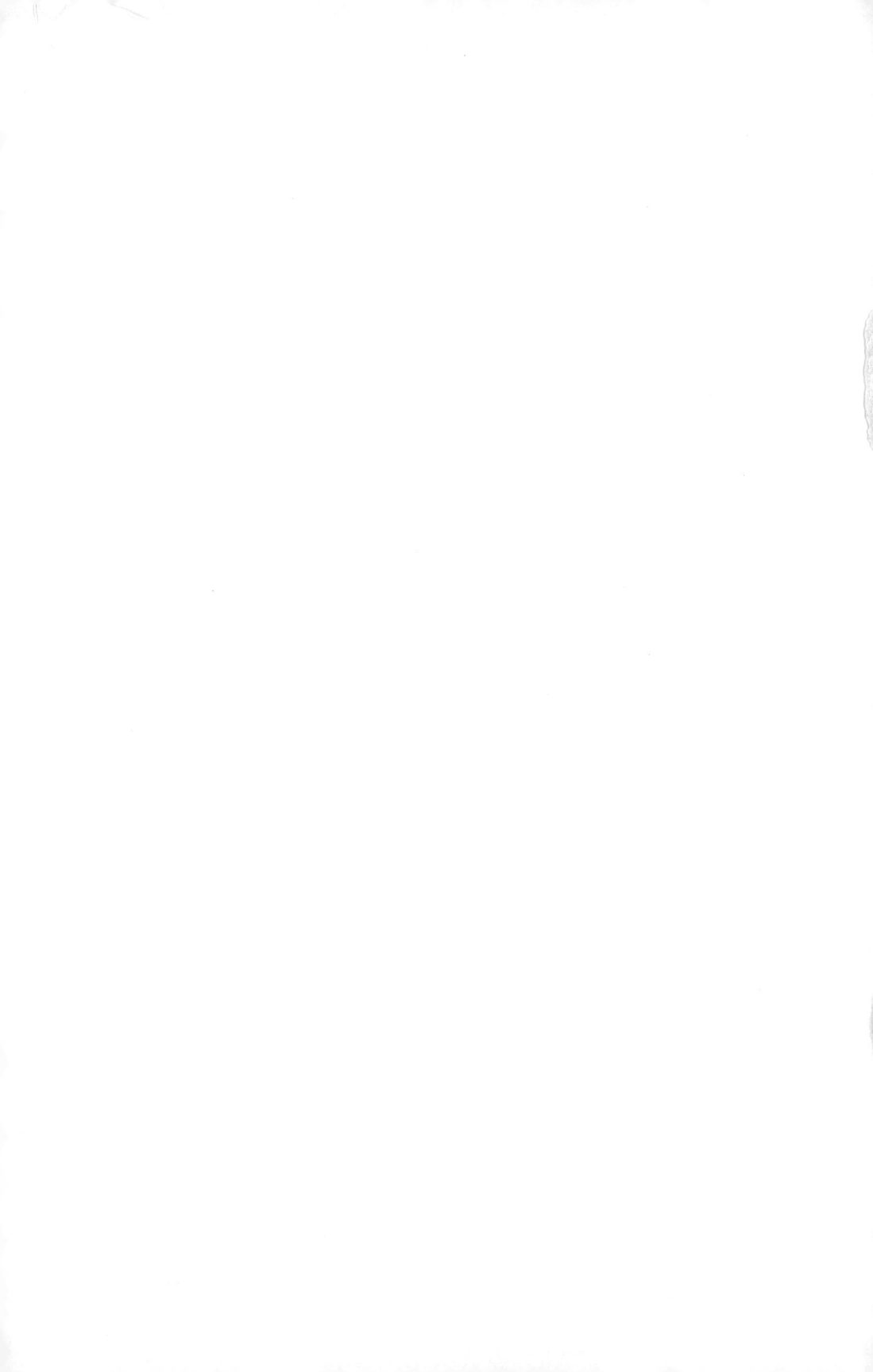

Table of Contents

SETUP AND EQUIPMENT 7-9AM
Needed time 2 hours

OBTAIN A PIANO.

For starters buying an actual piano to practice or keep on at home is highly recommended. Pianos vary broadly in style, cost, and size; for most individuals, a medium-sized standing piano is perfect, as it takes up a lesser amount of space than the grand piano and has better sound than most compact classes. Bear in mind that though it's possible to bargain pianos for cheap and at times even for free, it's dangerous and hard to move an upright from one position to another. Be certain you have a professional transport service lined up to aid you move your piano.

GETTING THE BEST DEAL

When you buy a used piano for less or no money on the market, it's likely you'll need to get it fine-tuned and possibly even restored before it is functional. Check your local listings to find somebody who's ready to make that house call and evaluate your piano's condition.

GETTING THE RIGHT KEYBOARD

It's conventional to buy a high-quality keyboard if you must (for instance if you stay in a tiny studio flat), but it isn't advisable. You'll have more difficult learning proper hand positioning and posture than you would with the actual piano, and you will never be able to exercise as much control over a sound of an electric keyboard as you will with a piano.

PROCURE ACCESSORIES 7-9 AM

Once the piano is set in the right position and has been fine-tuned and inspected by an expert, it's time to get a good bench and some tune to play. A lot of pianos come with a bench; if not, they can be bought at thrift stores or music stores. Try to acquire an adjustable bench, since bench height is important to ensuring a correct posture. Don't use a room chair or couch as a substitute except it places you at the perfect height for playing.

OBTAINING THE METRONOME.

If you have difficulty keeping a rhythm, purchase a metronome. The metronome sits on top your piano then ticks like a clock at a speed you set. It's a valuable aid for keeping a steady tempo as you start to get playing.

KEYBOARD HAND AND POSTURE POSITIONS
9-10 AM
Needed time 1-2 hours

CHECK YOUR HAND POSITION.

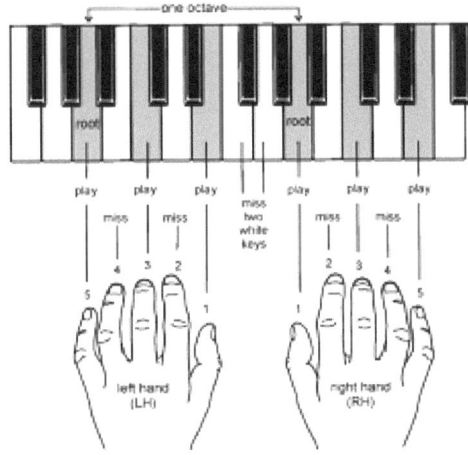

Take a seat on your piano bench with the music books on the piano sill, above the keyboard. Direct your forearms in the direction of the keys till they're parallel to the ground. If your piano bench is at the correct height, the fingers should arc downward and lay on the keys tops, without you bending your wrists or increase or lower your hands. Adjust the bench stature until you feel no pressure on your arms or the shoulders when you sit down at the piano.

THE FEET POSITION

Rest the feet flat on the floor, a relaxed distance apart, and the toes pointing ahead. Sit with your back straight - your shoulders shouldn't curve forward, and your spine ought to be straight. Scoot in till your hands rest well on the keys without stretching your arms. You ought to be able to move the feet forward to the piano pedals and back without putting any pressure on your upper feet.

FLEXIBLE PIANO BENCH

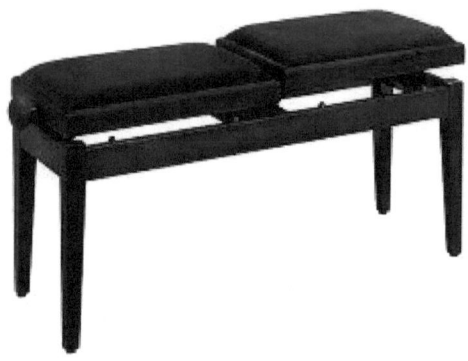

If you lack an adjustable bench, or it just won't adjust enough to make you at ease, it's acceptable to use pillows or pads to further raise the height of the seat. Just be certain they're even in thickness terms, and steady enough that you will not have to concern about them sliding as you play.

CHECK THE HAND POSITION.

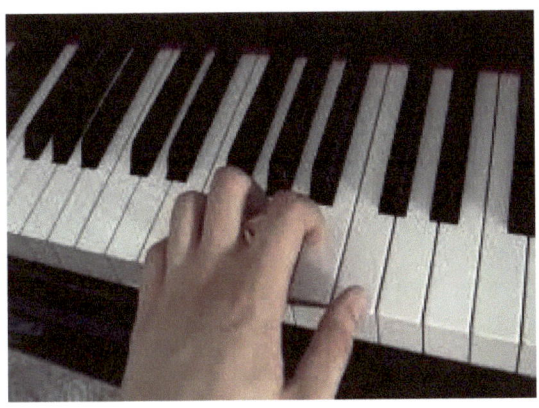

You ought to be seated in the middle of the keyboard. All of your ten fingers resting on 1 white key. Your right thumb is resting on the white key only to the left of the group of 2 black keys in the center of the keyboard that is the C keyboard note. Each finger on the right hand resting on the next white key, therefore D, E, F, then G. Your Left-hand following the same pattern 1 octave down, simply reversed: the left pinky rests on C note, and the left thumb rests on G. There should be 2 white keys (A or B) between the thumbs.

THE C KEYBOARD NOTE

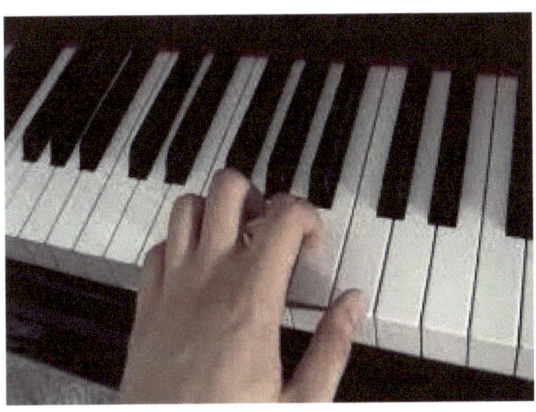

The C note anchors the right thumb is in the middle of the keyboard and is often known as "middle C." It's very common for novice players to use a piece of tape or a sticker to mark C note. Just be certain it's something you can finally clean off as you carry on well.

LEARNING THE CENTER NOTES

Learning the center notes first is conventional since a pianist must generally sit at the midpoint of the keyboard to reach every high or low note without moving and standing up.

BASIC PIANO KNOWLEDGE 10-11 AM

Needed time 1-2 hours

PIANO NOTES.

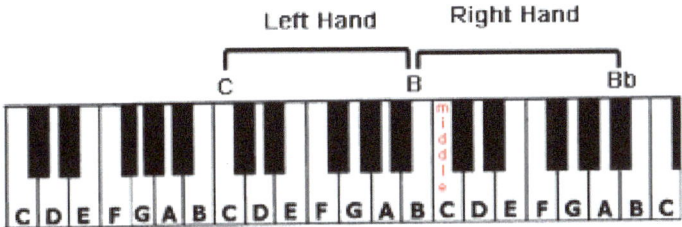

There are seven piano notes: C, D, E, F, G, A, B

Piano Keys. There are 88 piano keys on a keyboard. White keys are called natural keys because they make a more natural note if pressed. Black piano keys are known as accidentals since they make a flat or sharp note when pressed.

There are 7 naturals on the piano.

There are 5 accidentals per octave in addition they can be either sharp or flat.

PIANO CHORDS.

There are many piano chords which are in use. Four basic chords are minor, major, augmented and diminished.

THE SUPPLEMENTARY METHOD OF PIANO LESSONS

Learning keyboards.

These instruments light up in a particular order to aid you learn tunes more quickly, plus typically come with videos and books that will help you absorb musical notation.

a) DVD's and. Tapes

This technique is particularly useful for visual learners since you can see the harmony being played successfully.

b) Play by the ear.

This is questionably the most difficult technique, nonetheless can work if you have difficult learning musical note. Play the records over and over till you are able to repeat the melody.

PIANO TECHNIQUES AND THEORY
11-1 PM
Needed time 2 hours

LEARNING THE KEYBOARD

The piano keyboard repeats notes from bottom to top across a number of octaves. This implies that these notes change from the high (right side) to low (left side), but don't contrast in pitch. There are 12 notes a piano produces: 7 white key notes (From C, D, E, G, A, F, to B) and 5 black key notes (from C-sharp, D-sharp, the F-sharp, A-flat, to B-flat). Playing white key notes from C all through B and then back to C makes a even eight tone octave gauge in C major; in performance the black key notes at C-sharp (near the white C key) all through B-flat makes a (five tone) pentatonic scale. You can piece (both black and white) every key from C to the C to create a twelve-tone scale or chromatic.

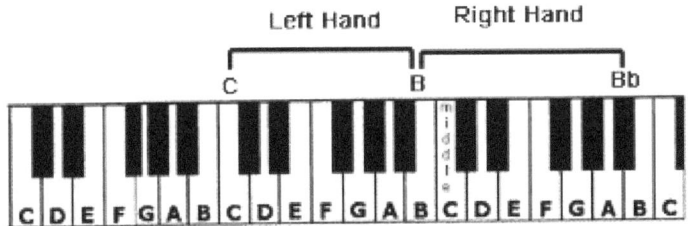

The piano is adjusted for C major, as it's a common key. However, the other keys are played by mixing the white and black keys to get the apt flats and sharps for each note. The keys normally in sheet music can be well played on a piano, enabling it to be viewed as a very versatile instrument.

It is easy to double-check the piano's fine-tuning by playing pairs of same note at several octaves. The notes ought to sound identical; one or both is sharp if they don't or flat and necessities to be re-tuned.

NOW PLAY SOME NOTES.

Beginning with middle C, firmly but gently push down on a white key to make a note. Take time then try pushing faster and slower, harder and softer, until you get an idea of the sort of control you can apply to the piano sound. Without shifting your hands, now play all 10 notes under your hand fingers. Notice that some (for instance the pinky) are more hard to play at full volume while others (such as the thumb) need some practice to play tenderly.

Play the black keys as well. The black keys are generally played by moving the proper finger up then to the right, bar in the case of a thumb, since it's hard to move the thumb up while you play a black key and not ruin your hand position. After the middle C point, your pointer finger should move left then right to play the C-sharp and the D-sharp, respectively.

NOW PLAY SCALES.

Try playing some notes starting with a pinky C of the Left-hand, to the thumb C of the right-hand. Press each white piano key in order. When you reach the left thumb, spring it to play the subsequent note up (A), then your right thumb to press the next (B), returning the thumb to center C to finish the scale. Continue practicing this until it starts to get easier – extending your fingers is as important as shifting your hands.

Try playing another scale. Start on the one of the opposite fingers of the Left-hand, and keynotes up the piano until you get the same note on the right-hand. Adjust the sour notes by with black keys where needed. This is exactly how other scales apart from the C major are played. For instance, D major scale is started by playing D (left ring finger), F-sharp (black key), E, G, A, C-sharp (the black key), B, D (right pointing finger).

Along with learning scales from this guidebook, it's imperative to keep trying with them on your own consequently that you start to understand them as fast as possible.

UNDERSTAND THE HARMONY.

Though it doesn't take much practice to play out "Hot Cross Buns" on a keyboard, unlocking your instrument's potential needs learning to play many notes at once, using all the fingers and both hands. To achieve a lovely sound with many notes, you have to appreciate how harmonies function. This is an in-depth subject that can't be fully covered in full here. However, you can apply these notes to aid guide your piano practice.

Neighboring notes never harmonize. It doesn't mean that they don't have a position in advanced compositions, for now, remember: pressing two notes next to each other seldom sounds good. The harmonies beam are shaped by increasing the distance between notes.

The distance between the harmony's notes is known as its "interval." The most well-known intervals in the piano music are thirds, fourths, and fifths. To hear samples of these, play a C and a G, a C and an F, or a C and an E, respectively.

Harmony intervals can up to the fourteenth interval, which is taken as a compound interval as it crosses more than a single octave. Harmonies may also be changed by introducing sharp or flat notes, including support notes, etcetera. However, you should not have to care too much about the more advanced styles yet.

Playing one note at two octaves is known as "unison" harmony.

The Steps are;

Steps

1. Choose if you wish to play piano or keyboard or both. The piano keys (or piano-styled keyboard keys) are "well weighted" which implies that the volume of sound it makes are determined by how firmly you hold each key. This is difficult at first though essential to understand if you wish to play with expression and feeling. It's very easy to play the keyboard having understood a piano, or a piano-styled keyboard, however, it's hard to grasp the piano style keys if you have only played the keyboard.
2. Manage your play time well. Continually use no less than 20 Minutes of your time to practice the piano. The more you play, the better you'll be! It's so obvious, but so true.
3. Begin the exercise with an easy tune you know well. (Top of the World, Fur Elise, etc.) You will probably be most acquainted with the melody, therefore, try out the top part first or right-hand.
4. Try to apply (do, re, mi, fa, so, la, ti, do) keys to fit the hums of the melody. (Sounds weird? I know, but assists) If not, try applying the sharp or "black" keys to fit the pitch. As you advance, try more difficult accompaniments as well.

5. Patience is the important part of learning a tune. Do not give up even after failing 10 times. Progressively you'll play with fewer and fewer mistakes till it's perfect.
6. Breathe while you play. Always notice the pitches. Be relaxed and calm. Do not play fast till you're totally sure you have got it.
7. Try with both hands when you have mastered the every part on its own. It doesn't happen overnight. For me, it took 7 days to harmonize Fur Elise fully.
8. Think of where the fingers go, try to discover the best method to play so the fingers don't get tangled up or cross over!

DEVELOPING YOUR PIANO SKILLS 2-4 PM

Needed time 2 hours

STUDY MUSIC THE SHEET

The sheet music language notation may seem hard at first, but with this guidebook and some rehearse, most people understand the basics in just a week. Ability to read sheet music unlocks up an entire world of compositions to learn and rehearse. Again, reading the sheet music is an involving procedure; however, the very fundamentals have been charted below for reference.

Heads

Music notes are characterized by empty or filled-in oval marks (known as heads), with or minus other marks (called stems, which are conventional lines, plus hooks, that are of stems) of a series of horizontal strokes known as a staff that begin on a certain note, which need to be memorized on the symbol or clef, in front of a staff. Different types of note signify different lengths. A head shorn of a stem is a full note, the lengthiest type; a filled head that has a stem or a hook is a one-eighth note and lasts an eighth the whole note.

Every note is positioned from left to the right in chronological arrangement, and from low to high based on how low or high on the piano is. Notes located along one vertical line are to be played together.

The notes are split into bars or measures, to add regularity and structure which are then noted by the vertical lines from the staff. Each bar is played in the same time length; thus, a few extended notes or many smaller notes fit into a given bar. However, they must at all times add up to the same total.

2 numbers near the clef at the begging of the music create the time signature. The time signature shows the length of note that can be played per bar. The popular 4/4-time signature, for instance, indicates that 4 quarter notes can be played per bar.

 "Rests" are special signs for pauses in play. Rests are written onto bars and read like notes.

REHEARSE USING YOUR BOTH HANDS INDEPENDENTLY.

Many compositions necessitate you to play a rhythm on one hand, and another rhythm on the other. In particular, the Left-hand will mostly be playing low notes, while the right-hand plays a higher melody. Similar to patting the head as you rub the stomach, this method takes some time to pick up. Rehearse by playing a tune with the right hand, and picking out whole note accords with your left.

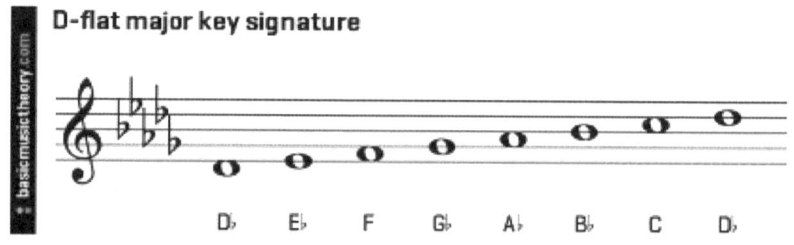

D-flat major key signature

REHERSE MOVING THE HANDS.

Eventually, you will have to leave the central C area of the keyboard then venture out to the edges. Be accustomed to the notion by sometimes picking out your practice training an octave higher or lower than normal. Be seated as normal, and don't bend down the piano bench – in a performance, you wouldn't get time to bend from the high end to low end the. Instead, bend your torso slightly from side to side (without twisting or bending your back), and contract or stretch your arms to get the notes.

Try shifting positions on the fly. Pick out something simple, such as a scale or an arpeggio, from a lesser position than normal, and jump the hands up to last it through a next octave. If you begin with the Left-hand, let it cross slightly over the right and hold location above the correct keys just as you need it for the next octave. As you pick out those notes, draw the right-hand back to a higher position too.

LEARNING HOW TO USE THE PEDALS.

Before the electric guitar, most pianos were applying effects pedals to shift the sound feature of the music from the strings. Two to 3 pedals can be found on most contemporary pianos, each has an important role. In classical masterpieces, a special notation is required to show when or how to apply which pedal.

On the left, you will find the soft pedal. It softens not both the volume, and the tone note color being played. This soft pedal is applied extensively in most Beethoven's compositions.

On the right is the sustaining pedal. It lifts the diminishing elements of the strings, letting notes to blend, resonate, and ring much more effortlessly. Clever application of the sustaining pedal could connect harmonies as well as notes in interesting and expressively evocative ways, plus it is commonly seen in masterpieces dating from the 19th century forward.

The third, middle pedal is the sostenuto pedal if found on a grand piano. A sostenuto sustains notes. However, it does so selectively, not across the board. On the upright piano, it's probable that the middle pedal (if there is one) is the mute pedal.

PRACTICE MORE.

A piano is among the most difficult instruments to play, but also among the most rewarding: the quality of sound it makes is impressive and distinctive, and the skills needed to play it well can easily transfer to any other instruments. The main thing to getting good at mastering the piano is to rehearse as much as you can, whenever possible. Purpose to devote no less than half an hour daily to playing it; when you can take one hour or more, that is even better. Though you may feel as is you are not making the needed headway, just practice more and everything will fall right into place.

REFINING YOUR SKILLS 4-5 PM
Needed time 1 hour

After you have mastered the basics, now it's time to advance your piano techniques.

Starting to understand piano but you are finding it hard to advance? Been to piano lessons for some time but feeling no improvement? Or perhaps you have a little piano experience, and you need to advance your playing skills?

I'll be showing you exactly how to improve your present piano skills. The eBook takes into account persons who learned playing piano by ear, using training materials such as DVDs and books, or using instructions from a professional piano guide. Dive in and have fun!

Steps

MANAGE YOUR PRACTICE AND LEARNING TIME.

Allocate a time slot to practice sessions or exercise and be committed to it. Try not to let anything to discourage you as you practice. Commitment to exercise is crucial to refining your abilities.

Use plans if your time is full and you can't periodically dedicate the same time slot.

Apply reminders on your device to remind you of your practice sessions.

PLAN YOUR PRACTICE.

Though this is not essential later, at the, when you are learning new skills, it's key to know what you are learning in the following few sessions to be able to size your progress. This is meant to help you track your skills and knowledge progress, do not be disappoint if you didn't have the progress you expected. If you feel a particular concept took a long time to play, don't worry. The key is that, eventually, you do know it.

ADVANCE YOUR MUSICAL NOTATION READING SKILLS.

Most of the tips and steps to follow will depend on or significantly benefit from an ability in reading sheet music or musical notation. Do as follows:

Learn to read sheet music if you haven't previously done so.

Ensure you understand many of the models of musical notation. If you wish to improve your general piano playing, you will need to learn more advanced harmonious notations like dynamics, time signatures, key and tempo, clefs, etc. Knowing just how to read these notes themselves or their intervals won't be sufficient.

Learn to sight-read sheet music.

This will advance your ability to convert what you can see and can understand on the sheet into lovely piano tunes.

Improve your finger speed and placement on the keyboard keys:

Learn finger stretching exercises to apply before you start playing.

Learn correct piano finger location if you haven't previously done so. Having your fingers properly on the keys is crucial to increasing more advanced abilities.

Practice the many scales using correct finger placement. Begin by practicing climbing up the scale, and down, then up as well as down. Do each at least 5 times using correct finger placement when performing a certain scale.

Attempt to practice 2 or 3 scales before every session. Do this in a "session" during a lesson with a piano guide, or at your free time slot you dedicated to practicing and learning the piano.

Try to rehearse using sheet music with finger numbering on them, principally. This way you are certain that you are mastering correctly.

Practice with an increasing speed. Set the metronome at a slower speed then when you have grasped one-speed interchange it up to another faster speed. This will advance muscle memory. While learning a new tune, or another scale, start by mastering it slowly but submitting to the timing of the tune. Then, begin speeding up, having proper time intervals in between the notes. For instance, if working on a simple C note Major scale, you will start by playing all notes (from C, D, E, F, G, A, all the way to B) as an entire beat. Then begin playing each for half a beat (and not leaving the remaining half beat with a rest), and then a quarter, etcetera. Once you make an error, start again. Practice for half an hour every day till you feel you are doing it without mistakes.

Practice chords finger positioning. You can find a lot section later in this guidebook detailing correct finger placement for every chord. Sometimes you'll discover more than one ideal finger placement; its jus a matter of preference, so adopt whichever placement technique that makes you more contented while playing (particularly while progressing from the first chord to the second).

Practice and memorize musical scales, particularly the most conspicuous ones. Pick up all the Major, choral minor, melodic minor as well as chromatic scales. Pick up the scales then practice them. Furthermore, if you're mastering a specific technique (such as the blues, jazz, and so on.), learn the style scales.

Practice and memorize chords. Chords are many notes played at the same time (on a piano, pressing several keys simultaneously).

Start by learning the prominent chords.

Learn the many inversions of a chord. Attempt to learn what time and in what progress each inversion is applied.

Practice chords by mastering progressions. Start with easy ones like the C-F-G progression. After you've grasped those, go to more complex ones.

Improve your musical ear (commonly called musical aptitude) by practicing paying attention to musical notes and trying to deduce their notes. To do this:

Start with slow and simple songs. Try to catch the notes of the tune first through trial and error on the piano.

Try to label the notes using just your ear, and write them down.

After you've done a section, try performing the notes you've noted down, see just how close you were.

You may create some grading manner and try to test yourself. Don't get worried if you get just a few notes at the beginning. Just learn from these mistakes you make. Then Bit by bit, you will someday write down the entire song with more accuracy.

Improve your instrumental "mind playing". This is when you master a piece or a song of music in the mind. This can be achieved as follows:

Look at a music sheet and try to master it in your mind. In the beginning, you'll find strain doing so, so master it tone by tone. In the initial stages, you might use some kind of recording device then read the notes by recording and humming. With progress, you'll begin recording bigger chunks of the music sheet before stopping to read the ensuing chunk. Then you are able to sightread entire passages, melodies, plus even pieces in your head.

After that, play the piece then see how close it is.

Make sure your piano posture is proper. Improper piano posture can cause back pain which consecutively makes your body stiffer so that you can't master as easily as you would if the posture were correct.

Align your pelvis opposite to the Middle C note.

Sit upright, not leaning towards or away from the keyboard.

Be relaxed, not stiff.

Your fingers should be slightly curved downwards as if you're holding an apple in you a hand. Do not position your fingers in a perpendicular position with the keys. Also, do not allow your fingers to curve upwards.

If you are new to playing, then watch out for the pinky fingers. They appear to go a bit higher than other fingers for novel learners. Try to style each pinky remain at the same flat as the rest. This might require some practice to start with, but keep it up till it becomes the normal stance.

Practice on your preferred musical songs or pieces at first. You will discover a lot of unrestricted sheet music online, and you can purchase song books or sheet music from a lot of music stores. You can moreover download midi files of the piece or song and transform it into a sheet music using a software for example MuseScore.

Start by mastering the piece really gradually. What matters in the beginning is that you get the progress of chords and notes.

The concern with timing at the next phase. After you've grasped the development and progressions of the song, start improving your timing. Ensure each note is mastered for the period it is destined to be played, as well as at the time needed.

Use sectioning as you learn. Learn the sections of the piece, play them then move to the subsequent section. The section can be a chorus, a chord progression, a melody or a refrain, and so on.

Improve your right-hand left-hand coordination abilities. This can be done as follows:

Do some harmonization exercises before you begin practicing. The application of a metronome would be good so long as you can practice harmonization at different tempos.

While practicing more compound pieces, start by performing the Left-hand portion of a piece, before the right-hand (or vice versa) before you try to play them all together. Take your time and don't rush it. After you've played one portion, move onwards to the next part, not before that.

Practice performance in public. It's significant to get accustomed playing in the open and not getting tense due to a wrong note or chord.

Start by playing in front of a lesser group of private associates (family, friends, etc.).

Increase the attendants slowly.

Start playing in private events (picnics, retreats, parties, etc.)

Make use of contemporary technology in case you are performing by yourself. There is a broad range of hardware and software designed to help in the improvement and practicing process.

Some of are:

The metronome devices. Applied to practice tempo and timing and regulate your playing in harmony with time.

The software pianos. These are useful while refining your musical aptitude as well as mind reading.

Musical symbolization software for instance MuseScore. This kind of software is useful for converting midi files to sheet music. It is useful for storing melodic scores digitally, reprinting them, managing them, etc. Furthermore, software aids with the practice of composing tunes.

Practice aids and musical software games such as PrestoKeys and Synthesia. These aids and games are used to exercise musical notches by using a piano or a MIDI keyboard (in which case, the aid won't keep your score).

Learn the finger placement techniques. Efficient finger placement will help your practice so much more. Liken this to multiplication. For example, you were given the mathematical problem 6 plus 6 plus 6 a hundred times, would you 5 * 100 or do 5 + 5 + 5 +...? Obviously the first option. Likewise, if you use a more efficient finger placement, why not practice it? It takes one minute extra to work out what finger placement fits you best. One minute spent at the present could save you days later when you attempt to change your finger placement.

Know how your hand muscles work. Mostly this comes from a common logic. For instance, you can effortlessly figure out something with the index finger. How about the ring finger (thumb translates to 1, index translates to 2, middle translates to 3, ring, translates to 4, pinkie translates to 5) I'm not a professional in human anatomy, nonetheless it's likely that a thumb and the index finger have separate muscles, whereas the third, fourth and fifth fingers have muscles linked to each other. Consequently, don't use agonizingly painful fingering, for instance pressing the center C with the pinkie then for the E key with the thumb and the G with the ring finger.

Buy a sheet music. In case you can afford the sheet music, it in your best interests to buy one so. Sheet music has finger positioning (only the positioning you need to be acquainted with), and people will have tested it before bundling it in the copy. You can copy books as well, but ensure you don't infringe any copyright laws.

PLAYING MAJOR PIANO CHORDS 5-9 PM

Needed time 4 hours

Piano chord is what makes the music inspiring and gives it character. They are the most basic and key things for every single pianist to be acquainted with, and they're easy to learn! I'll show you the rules, and then let you go rehearse!

CHORD BASICS

What is a chord?

A chord is 3 or more notes. Compound chords may have a lot of notes, but you require a minimum of 3.

The chords outlined here will all be made up of 3 notes: a root, a fifth and a third.

Playing the chord root.

Each major chord is put together on a note known as the tonic or chord root. This is the musical note that a chord is christened after and is the lowest note found in a chord.

For the C major chord, the C becomes the tonic. It is placed on the bottom note of the chord.

You then will play a tonic note with the thumb in the right-hand, or with the pinkie in your hand.

Playing the major third.

The next note in another major chord the third major, which offers the chord character. It is four half-steps or semitones, above a root. It is known as a third since when you play the scale in that music key, it is the third note that a pianist hits.

29

For the C major chord, an E is the third. It's four half steps over C. Counting them from your piano the number you get is four, namely; (from C#, D, D#, to E).

Regardless of the hand you're playing using will pick up the third by the middle finger.

To get a feeling of how that intermission is thought to sound attempt playing the third and the root together.

Playing the fifth.

The upper note in another major chord is known as the fifth because whenever you pick up the scale it is the fifth note you hit. It supports the chord and completes it. It is 7 semi-tones above the chord root.

For the C major chord, a G is the fifth. A player can count the 7 semi-tones from the piano root. (from C#, D, D#, all the way E, F, F#, to G.)

You pick up the fifth with the pinkie in the right-hand, or the thumb on the left.

Know that there are as a minimum two techniques of spelling a chord.

All the notes can be printed at least 2 different ways, for instance the Eb and the D# are one and the same note. Therefore, the Eb major chord should sound like the D# major chord.

The music notes Bb, Eb, G, create the Eb chord. The music notes F□ (F##), D#, A# make a D# Major chord, this sounds precisely like the Eb chord.

The 2 chords are known as enharmonic equivalents since they sound precisely the same even though they are printed differently.

A small number of-of the popular enharmonic equivalents are mentioned below, but otherwise the eBook presents only the most popular notation of the major chord.

Review correct hand position.

So as to play a tone of piano composition well, you must consistently use the right-hand placement, even when you are just performing chords.

Keep the fingers tall and bent, like they are leaping into the keys. Apply the natural arc of your fingers.

Apply the weight of the arms rather than the power of the fingers to drive on the piano keys.

Play on your fingers tips, if possible the thumb and the pinkie which have a habit of lying flat if you are not paying concern.

Have your fingernails trimmed down so that you will easily play using your fingertips?

PLAYING THE CHORDS

1. Using 3 fingers.
Note that you only use fingers (thumb, middle, pinkie) 1, 3 and 5 to play the 3 notes of every chord. Your ring and index fingers can rest on, but not hold down the keys.

Note that your fingers spread 1 half-step (1 key) up the piano keyboard every time you shift chords.

2. Playing the C Major.

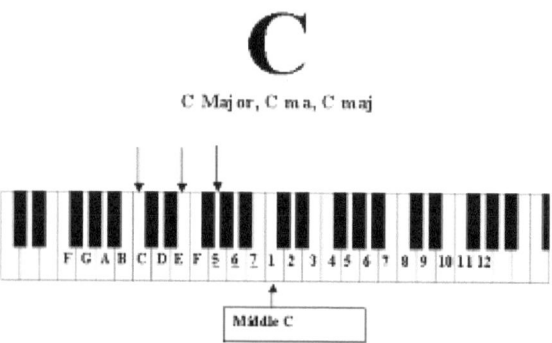

The 3 notes are E, C, G. Remember, C translates to (0) tonic, E translates to (4 semi-tones) major third, G translates to (7 semi-tones) fifth.

Right-hand finger placement will position the thumb on C, the middle finger on the E and the pinkie on the G.

Left-hand finger placement will position the pinkie on C, the middle finger on E and the thumb on G.

3. Playing the Db Major.

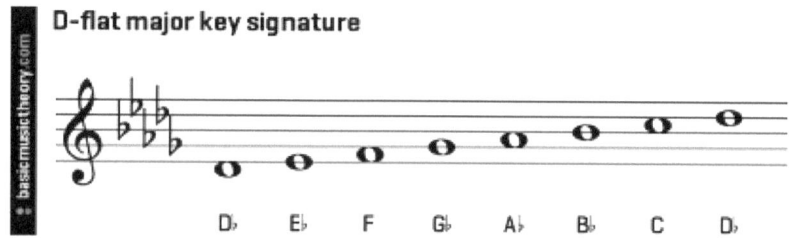

The 3 notes are Ab, F, Db. Remember, Db translates to tonic (0), F translates to (4 semi-tones) major third, Ab translates to (7 semi-tones) fifth. The enharmonic equal of this chord is the C# Major. Note that Db can also be presented as C#. F may also be inscribed in music as the E#. Ab may also be inscribed as G#. The follow-ups you play are the same whether it's written as a Db Major or a C# Major.

Right-hand finger placement will position the thumb on Db, the middle finger on the F and the pinkie on Ab.

The Left-hand finger placement will position the pinkie on Db, the middle finger on the F and the thumb on Ab.

4. Playing D Major.

The 3 notes are A, F#, D. Remember, D translates to tonic (0), F# translates to (4 semi-tones) major third, A translates to (7 semi-tones) fifth.

Right-hand finger placement will position the thumb on D, the middle finger at F# and pinkie at A.

Left-hand finger placement will position a pinkie at D, the middle finger at F# and the thumb at A.

5. Playing Eb Major.

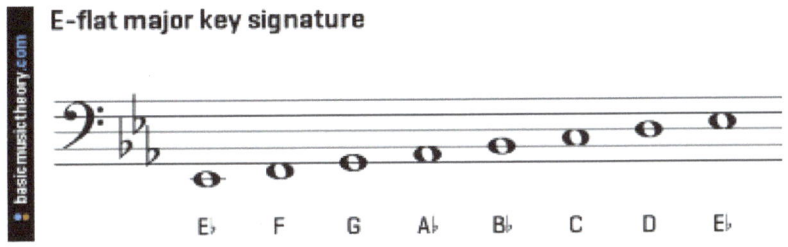

The 3 notes are Bb, G, Eb. Remember, Eb translates to tonic (0), G translates to (4 semi-tones) major third, Bb translates to (7 semi-tones) fifth.

Right-hand finger placement will position the thumb at Eb, the middle finger at G and the pinkie at Bb.

Left-hand finger placement will position the pinkie at Eb, the middle finger at G and the thumb at Bb.

6. Playing E Major.

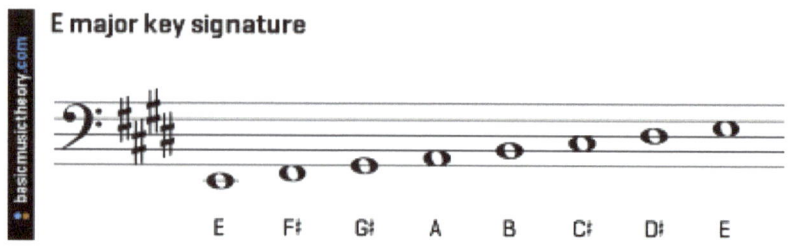

E major key signature

E   F♯   G♯   A   B   C♯   D♯   E

The 3 notes are B, G#, E. Remember, E translates to tonic (0), G# translates to major third (4 semi-tones), B translates to fifth (7 semi-tones).

Right-hand finger placement will position the thumb on E, the middle finger on G# and the pinkie on B.

Left-hand finger placement will position the pinkie on E, the middle finger on G# and the thumb on B.

7. Play F Major.

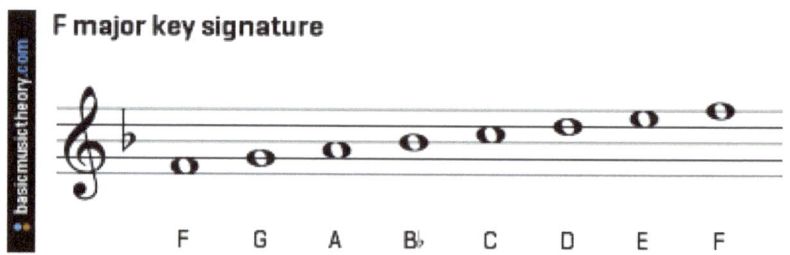

F major key signature

F   G   A   B♭   C   D   E   F

The 3 notes are F, A, C. Remember, F translates to tonic (0), A translates to major third (4 semi-tones), C translates to fifth (7 semi-tones).

Right-hand finger placement will position the thumb on F, the middle finger on A and the pinkie on C.

Left-hand finger placement will position the pinkie on F, the middle finger on A and the thumb on C.

8. Play F# Major.

The 3 notes are F#, A#, C#. Remember, F# translates to tonic (0), A# translates to major third (4 semi-tones), C# translates to fifth (7 semi-tones). The enharmonic equal of this chord is Gb Major, which are written as Gb, Bb, Db. Note that F# can be presented as Gb. A# can be presented as Bb. C# can be presented as Db. Therefore the notes you pick up to make this major chord are the same in F# Major and Gb Major.

Right-hand finger placement will position the thumb on F#, the middle finger on A# and the pinkie on C#.

Left-hand finger placement will position the pinkie on F#, the middle finger on A# and the thumb on C#.

9. Play G Major.

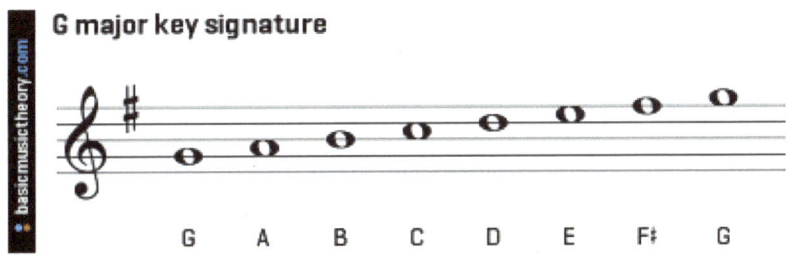

The 3 notes are G, B, D. Remember, G translates to tonic (0), B translates to major third (4 semi-tones), D translates to fifth (7 semi-tones).

Right-hand finger placement will position the thumb on G, the middle finger on B and the pinkie on D.

Left-hand finger placement will position the pinkie on G, the middle finger on B and the thumb on D.

10.Play Ab Major.

The 3 notes are Ab, C, Eb. Remember, Ab translates to tonic (0), C translates to major third (4 semi-tones), Eb translates to fifth (7 semi-tones). The enharmonic equal of this chord is G# Major, which are written as G#, B#, D#. Note that Ab can be presented as G#. C can be presented as B#. Eb can be presented as D#. The notes you play to make a major chord are the same for Ab Major and G# major, although they are noted differently.

Right-hand finger placement will position the thumb on Ab, the middle finger on C and the pinkie on Eb.

Left-hand finger placement will position the pinkie on Ab, the middle finger on C and the thumb on Eb.

11.Play A Major.

The 3 notes are A, C#, E. Remember, A translates to tonic (0), C# translates to major third (4 semi-tones), E translates to fifth (7 semi-tones).

Right-hand finger placement will position the thumb on A, the middle finger on C# and the pinkie on E.

Left-hand finger placement will position the pinkie on A, the middle finger on C# and the thumb on E.

12.Play Bb Major.

The 3 notes are Bb, D, F. Remember, Bb translates to tonic (0), D translates to major third (4 semi-tones), F translates to fifth (7 semi-tones).

Right-hand finger placement will position the thumb on Bb, the middle finger on D and the pinkie on F.

Left-hand finger placement will position the pinkie on Bb, the middle finger on D, and the thumb on F.

13. Play B Major.

The 3 notes are B, D#, F#. Remember, B translates to tonic (0), D# translates to major third (4 semi-tones), F# translates to fifth (7 semi-tones).

Right-hand finger placement will position the thumb on B, the middle finger on D# and the pinkie on F#.

Left-hand finger placement will position the pinkie on B, the middle finger on D# and the thumb on F#.

PRACTICING

1) Rehearse playing all 3 notes simultaneously.

When you feel at ease playing all chords individually, try jumping up the scale with all the major chord. Start with the C major chord, and then master a Db major, and then master D major etcetera.

Begin this exercise by doing with only one hand. As soon as you feel assured, play two hands at once.

Listen for the false notes. The ratio of the notes should at all times remain the same, so if 1 chord suddenly sounds strange, review to see if you are striking the correct notes.

2) Arpeggios.

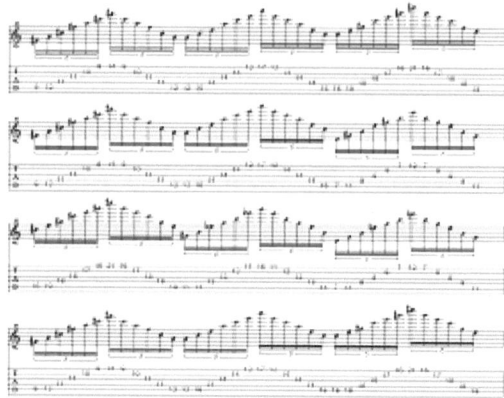

An arpeggio is after each note is hit in sequence from the lowest to the highest. To play the C Major arpeggio with the right-hand, strike the C with a thumb then release. Strike an E with the central finger then release. Hit G with a pinkie then release.

After you have grasped this motion, attempt to make it solid rather than rough. Strike and release every note quickly, subsequently there is scarcely sometime between notes.

Rehearse playing all the major chords in diverse inversions.

Chord Inversions use the same notes though position a separate note at the bottom. For instance, C major chord is G, E, C. The first C-major chord inversion is C, G, E. The second C-major inversion is C, E, G.

Test yourself by creating a major chord with each note up the scale, in all inversion.

Look out for chords in the sheet music. After you are at home with how to create and play a chord, practice a music piece with chords written. Look to tell if you can recognize major chords you have accomplished.

WHY YOU SHOULD START A PIANO LESSON TODAY

There are a number of benefits of playing the piano that are far beyond a bigger appreciation for music or the achievement of a new skill. Many of these benefits are valid for both children and adults– it's never too early, nor too late, to discover your musical side! In case you are still hesitant about signing up for some piano lessons, check out the following long-term benefits you can anticipate to reap.

1. Better Reaction to Criticism

It's important to see with a qualified pianist who will give you enough constructive criticism. When younger learners see their coach as a professional in the field, it's greatly easier to yield their advice and criticism. And this capacity to respond to disapproval – then learn from it – is typically carry over to other of daily life aspects, for example, work, and school.

2. Improved Capacity to Handle Stress

Joining piano recitals, or even performing in front of friends, can assist students deal with stage fright. Plus, all of the performing leading up to the concert will help you absorb goal-setting dedication and the self-discipline process.

3. Learn to Respond Well to Disappointments and Successes

This is another talent you will attain from performing, particularly if you take part in piano competitions. Comparable to knowledge on how to respond to disapproval, you may get some disappointment as you learn. A good piano guide will help you absorb how to keep a positive viewpoint, even when stuff doesn't go your way. When they go your way, you can rejoice your wins collectively!

4. Increased Communal Participation

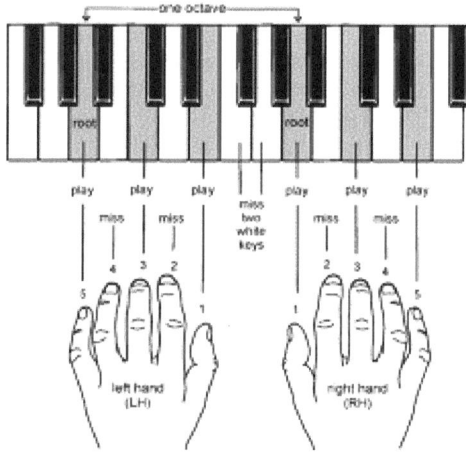

The –aptitude to a piece in front of friends is an important socializing skill. It's a good way to share your gifts with others, besides you may find yourself growing your network since you place yourself out in the musical community. Chatting your piano playing techniques with other players is a wonderful method to advance your comprehension of the instrument – and above, you never know how these connections will help you in life later!

5. Tougher Hand Muscles

Playing Piano is useful for developing agility in children as well as for maintaining forte in adult hands. Bear in mind, though: for the hand muscles to grow properly, you will need to learn the right form and hand placement for playing the keyboard with an expert guide.

6. Improved College Performance

Studies have established that children who start learning piano in grade school have healthier spatial and general cognitive growth than their peers; this can help improve their arithmetic skills. Furthermore, playing piano helps with concentration and consequently improve students' general class performance.

7. Aural Cognizance

Whether you obviously have a good nous of the pitch, playing piano can certainly help you advance. Some of these profits of piano playing include evolving a sense of virtual pitch, and exercising your mind to distinguish chords, intervals, and tones, which can assist with learning the music theory later in your studies.

8. Split Awareness

When you are first beginning to know how to play piano, it can be exceedingly frustrating to harmonize your two hands respectively playing something unlike. However the more you practice and play, the simpler it will get, trust me! Even the simpler pieces will teach you the abilities and focus you will need to advance your skills.

Split attentiveness is not only a physical skill; you can also practice the skill for pay attention. If you're taking piano lessons, you'll likely know how to heed to your playing sound both as if you are in the front of the hall and at the back room. You can apply the mental portion of this exercise in daily life to develop your multitasking abilities.

Final Notes

If you are been uncertain about embracing piano lessons for your child or yourself, think of all of these profits of playing the piano. Obviously, many people elect to start piano lessons for the simple pleasure of learning and mastering a music instrument as a hobby. What so ever your reason for beginning to play, know that you can start learning piano at any age. Put in the energy, and you'll note the positive outlooks you get when you acquire a new skill!

I hope that this book has challenged you and equip you with everything you were looking for within piano playing. Now that you have managed to learn these skills the next step to take now continue to playing and repeating these steps over and over again, challenge yourself to play without notes so you will craft your new skill, increase your pace and grow confidence.

www.ingramcontent.com/pod-product-compliance
Lightning Source LLC
Chambersburg PA
CBHW041111180526
45172CB00001B/202